SAUNDERSTOWN

SAUNDERSTOWN

DAVID OSBORN

DAGMAR
MIURA
LOS ANGELES

Published by Dagmar Miura
Los Angeles
www.dagmarmiura.com

Saunderstown

This book is a memoir. It reflects the author's present recollec-
tions of experiences over time.

First published 2025

ISBN: 979-8-89195-079-5

Contents

Six short adventures of my childhood summers ninety-five years ago when I was the same age as my grandchildren, Isobel and Ethan Warwick, are now remembered and written especially for them.

Preface

First, and just to get started, kids, where and what is Saunderstown? Well, ninety-five years ago it was a tiny string of small houses in the state of Rhode Island in the Northeast of the United States and was right on the edge of Narragansett Bay, a long narrow body of water that opens out onto the Atlantic Ocean. You can probably pull up a satellite map on your iPads.

Now where you will see a proper village with a church and all, back then in my childhood, there were only a few scattered houses each side of narrow Ferry Road that came down to a ferry slip or dock from a tiny post office on a main north-to-south highway. Near the ferry, a dirt road known as the Waterway, which hugged the shore of Narragansett Bay and had only two houses on it, went off into open countryside. One of those houses was my grandparents, where my brother Bayard and I spent the summer months, and it was the starting point for all our adventures.

Introduction

My grandparents? Wow, that was way back. Right? I don't know quite when they were born but let's talk first about my grandmother. She was then already white-haired, so it had to be in the 1800s.

Her name was Florence La Farge. Her father, Benoni Lockwood, was the captain of the *Bombay,* the last of the great three-masted clipper ships which sailed from New York to India and China. There were no steamships then. She was relatively poor, her shabby old two story house with its one-room tower, its gray-brown shingles weathered by salt air, was separated from the water only by a wide lawn and a small pier out into the bay with a float at its end that we swam from.

Grandma was a fabulous lady who spoke five languages. When young, she had rejected

marriage offers from several British titles, one a viscount, in favor of our grandfather, and she knew many important people, like the President of the United States, who didn't care how old and shabby her home. They came to see her.

An example: one early morning, I came into the living room, where she had her big cluttered desk, and saw a strange-looking old woman in weird golden clothes asleep on the couch, almost the only furniture there. Another in far less finery, and clearly her servant, was lying on the floor at her feet.

Guess what, and no kidding, it's true. She was the Empress of China with her servant. Arriving long after my grandparents had gone to bed and on finding the front door unlocked, they had simply walked in with all their baggage and had gone to sleep themselves.

Thursday afternoons always saw the Waterway a gridlock of Model T Fords and horses and buggies. It was when Grandma read from the classics on the wide veranda surrounding the house to ladies, all in their Sunday best finery, come from all over.

We kids weren't allowed on the property

DAVID OSBORN

then but sneaked a look from hiding in bushes across a little fish pond. I remember her reading aloud in Italian to rapt listeners from Dante's *Divine Comedy*.

The lawn was also the scene of endless croquet matches with notable gentlemen against whom Grandma was merciless. Croquet, played with wooden mallets and hard-as-rock composite the size of oranges, needed a big lawn for the multiple wickets a player had to pass through on their way to a final stake, while endlessly blocked from doing so by an opponent.

Few knew of Grandma's other life, where without drawing attention to herself, she was like an angel of mercy who often visited poor South County families, helping the midwife deliver a baby, washing their dirty linen and the bodies of the dying, cooking meals for the infirmed.

All that was your great-great-grandmother, Florence, and the very essence of my summers in Saunderstown.

Great, great, you are saying? Yes, I know that seems a long time back, but remember all I write about Saunderstown happened when I was just getting to be ten.

6

But what about your great-great-grand-father, Grant, a brilliant architect famous for the construction of St. John's Cathedral in New York, the largest in the New World, and that included all of North and South America, and larger than any in Australia, and many other important churches and government buildings.

Oddly, though, Grandpa was a devoted outdoorsman. To me, I most remember how he moved around, always silent. He padded about in Indian moccasins, without making a sound, and then you would suddenly find him right next to you without ever hearing him get there. He learned to do that from the years he had spent in the Pacific Northwest exploring the Columbia River, hunting and trapping, with an Indian friend from Maine and living entirely off the land.

At Saunderstown, he kept a small cabin sailboat, *The Windy-go*. We kids called it *The Golly Wog, wog* being a forbidden word. It was anchored near the float where we swam and where we kept our own stubby little canoe and three-person flat-bottom skiff. When you could learn to swim from the float to the shore, you were allowed to take either the skiff or the canoe out onto the Bay.

So, now on to the always inseparable company of your great-uncle Bayard, who was my brother. Bigger than me, although but a year older, he was far stronger and had a deceptively quiet manner that masked endless determination, which somehow matched his usually unkept dark short hair. One day he would become a famous artist, and meantime he was afraid of nothing. Not surprisingly, he was the US World War II Third Army boxing champion.

With us also was a lifelong friend, a roly-poly, full of fun, devil-may-care boy named Taylor Belcher whose father was a retired Army colonel and ran the coal company at Garrison, New York, where we had our permanent home.

Grandma believed that boys in particular had enough intelligence to look after themselves. For her, the test was if they were old enough and strong enough to climb up a drain pipe onto the roof and through a window into her bedroom. Then they could have breakfast coffee in bed with her, and they were on their own, free from any babysitters or grown-up supervision in whatever they did.

But they still had to abide by the simple rules of the house, which meant good manners and being home in time for dinner. (Girls? My grandmother felt the same. When my mother was growing, she had three brothers, and was driven to do everything her brothers did, from climbing the tallest tree to perching on slippery rooftops).

The three of us, Bayard, Taylor, and me, thus had endless adventures. What follows is the first of them.

Riding the Ferry for Free

F rom Saunderstown you can see the island of Jamestown, which fills most of Narragansett Bay before it opens into the Atlantic Ocean at famed Beavertail Lighthouse. It is only half mile from the mainland, but before they built a highway you could only reach Jamestown, and the famous wealthy resort of Newport beyond, it by ferry.

I can just barely remember when the ferry was driven by a huge paddlewheel. I was very young. But, by the time I was ten, it had been replaced by a ferry with a propeller and a deck that would take on four cars. It was that more modern ferry that my brother proposed we cross to Jamestown on.

But not exactly "on." Instead Bayard's plan

was to go "under," where iron poles from right beneath the car deck slanted down to just above the water.

"We'll sneak into the ferry slip on our canoe and skiff and paddle under the ferry," Bayard said, "then grab hold of the poles and get towed across the bay to Jamestown. Easy-peasy."

No sooner said and done, but as it turned out, hardly easy.

With Bayard in our little canoe and Taylor and I in an our equally small skiff, we sneaked under the ferry just as it was ready to cross the bay and grabbed onto the poles, Bayard in the canoe in front, Taylor and me in the skiff close behind.

Were we prepared for the jerk and violent swirl of water the moment cars were loaded and the ferry whistle blew announcing its departure? No. Both canoe and the skiff were instantly half swamped with water. We were frantically hanging on for dear life and had hardly left the ferry slip and were out onto the bay when the current tore the canoe away and Bayard was left clinging desperately to his pole, his legs dragging in the water that rushed by.

I try not to remember the rest of that dreadful trip, Bayard clinging, Taylor and I doing likewise to keep the bouncing-about skiff from completely capsizing. It seemed forever before we finally reached Jamestown, and Bayard was able to let go of his bar and drop into the skiff with Taylor and me.

But was the free ferry ride finally over? No way. What about the return? A furious ferry captain, learning of our hitchhiking, had sailors haul all three of us on deck so he could shout his fury that we had jeopardized his command. What discipline would he face if we had all drowned?

The upshot? We were put back into a bailed-out skiff and told that how we got home was our business.

And it was. And our business turned out to be a very long row. Wind and stiffened waves bounced us about. The skiff shipped in water again as we rowed and rowed. And bailed. It felt like forever. But eventually we made it, drenched and exhausted.

On the way we passed little Dutch Island, where during the long passed Spanish-American War, a battery of big guns had been established to prevent any enemy from coming up the bay. The island, with its long dark lighthouse and line of big guns, was a barren place occupied only by one poor lonely soldier, there to keep whatever in order but often too drunk to care. He lived in a small military house on the Jamestown side of Dutch Island.

We all resolved to visit the island next and examine those guns.

ADVENTURE TWO

▼

The Coastal Defense Cannon

We all had long been curious about Dutch Island, siting silently in the middle of the bay. A real challenge.

And it was easy enough to reach. Just half the distance to Jamestown Island, it was covered with gorse and bushes but not a single tree. There was a sort of rough beach at the opposite end to the long dark little lighthouse, and at a high point above it, two big concrete gun emplacements, each with two giant long-range cannons placed there to protect distant Providence during the Spanish-American Caribbean War in the late 1800s.

Undaunted, we skiffed over one day, all three of us, and climbed up to the guns. And wow, they were really big. Their twenty-foot-long barrels, ready to be raised or swung right and left, peered out from their platforms with their hand-cranked wheels to move and point them.

The lonely caretaker soldier might occasionally have been drunk, but he'd taken good care of them, as we soon found out. Taylor wasted no time in tackling a first gun, raising and lowering the long barrel with a well-oiled hand crank, and Bayard and I followed suit with the other gun.

But where were the shells they once shot? Fides was the one to find them. Fides, Latin for "faithful," was our big black Labrador. Bayard's sixth birthday present, he went everywhere with us, even to getting stuck halfway up a cliff at Bull Hill back in Garrison, New York. Try swimming alone? No way. Fides would dive in, grab any part of you he could, and retrieve you.

His barking brought me, then the others, to discover a whole row of well-preserved long range shells in a room in the concrete shelter. Big shiny things about four feet long, each contained enough gunpowder to shoot for miles the explosive projectiles capping them.

Awesome! The three of us were looking

down on the shells when we were startled by a gruff voice. "Where the devil did you kids come from?" And before any of us could catch our breaths, "Stop right where you are and don't touch."

We all froze, of course, each one of us vividly imagining the soon appearance of more soldiers, arrests, being dragged off to a military base, with an alarmed grandmother wondering where we were, and as night fell getting more and more worried.

It wasn't to be. To our general disbelief, there was sudden cackled laughter from the soldier. "Been doing a bit of exploring, have you? Shifting the guns about. Well, no harm in that. You might have learned something you could use someday, God forbid."

And then, as we simply stared in disbelief, "Did you find the light?"

"Light? What light?"

It didn't take long for us to find out. Still disbelieving, still expecting arrest, we obediently followed the soldier. "A sergeant," came in a whisper from Taylor, who knew these things because his father was a retired colonel.

We were herded like submissive sheep to where some tracks led to a big wooden shed.

Our captor flung the door open, revealing a giant military searchlight, the big glass face of which could have covered Grandma's house.

"We'll light it up," the gruff-sounding sergeant said, "but you must promise not to look at it when I do. You'll be blinded." He wrapped his scarf around Fides's head so Fides couldn't see. "Goes for the dog too."

The searchlight trundled out on its two tracks, the sergeant threw a switch, and suddenly the whole Saunderstown shore across the bay lit up like strong extra daylight, Grandma's house included.

There are kindly people here and there like that surprisingly friendly sergeant, but you don't run into them often. Putting the searchlight back, he took us down-island to the lighthouse, taking us up a spiraling outdoor stair to the top to explain how it worked before finally returning us to our beached skiff. "Don't tell nobody I showed you around," he said, and was gone.

Strange Voices from Afar and Almost Losing Fides

I t was a day I could never forget. One first filled with wonder, then with terror. It started late one afternoon near sunset, and the three of us, Bayard and Taylor and me, doing mostly nothing except lounging in the skiff somewhere in the middle of the bay. Grandma had resumed her regular Thursday readings, this time Milton's *Paradise Lost* in faultless English, until after a brief interlude, when to the delight of us boys, a horse broken loose from its buggy on the Waterway appeared. We watched, laughing, as it was being chased around the croquet lawn, of all places, by flower-hatted ladies in long gowns.

Fides was the first to hear the voices, then Bayard. The strange deep voices of men singing. Or was it chanting?

They came from near the Beavertail Lighthouse where the bay became the Atlantic Ocean. Rowing that way to get a closer look, we saw a ship that Taylor said was an oceangoing trawler. Behind it were two big barges as long as the ship itself.

"Angola," Taylor said, as we got much closer and could pick out strange words. "That's Africa. I bet they're fishermen. Come to fish the Grand Banks way up north."

And he was right. Big ivory-black men on the barges were hauling in nets filled with wriggling fish.

We got closer, the men saw us, and with deep throaty laughs, waved and kept on singing.

And then it happened, I'm not sure how. As the big mother ship began to go away, we seemed pulled in between the two barges, which at first didn't worry us because they were quite far apart.

But they didn't stay apart. They moved together faster and faster as the big trawler towing them picked up steam.

We couldn't do anything and were terrified as we three in our skiff got caught between the coming-together barges, first slammed back and forth and then thrown in the water, frantically grabbing onto any rope or net hanging from either barge.

There were huge roars of laughter from atop the barges. Big dark-skinned hands grabbed each one of us to safety. But what about Fides? All I could see was his helpless black head as the barges came together with a crash, to crush him.

But didn't. A miracle! One last powerful hand appeared from nowhere to snatch him free, and there he was, up on the barge as though nothing had happened, wagging his tail and shaking off water.

With their deep beautiful voices filling the air, singing, the ship with its barges moved away, back toward Angola. We three were given our rescued skiff, and piling into it with Fides, began the row back toward Grandma and the horse chase on the croquet lawn.

All about Eliza, not Fides

I had a day when I found myself alone. Summer was drawing to an end. Bayard had gone off to some art class, and Taylor had returned home to get ready for school.

I don't know what on earth got into me. It was so very long ago now. I left Grandma at her desk answering letters with a pen and ink, as was the way with everybody back in those days. People wrote letters. Finished writing, she'd blot the inked page, fold the paper, and put it in an envelope to be sealed with wax and stamped firmly shut with her personal stamp. Back then there were no computers with their texting and emails, and very few telephones, two-piece things, a receiver to hold to your ear and an upright thing to speak into. A crank on a wall box made it ring someplace where a woman's voice, the operator, asked you what number you wanted.

One of our uncles had put a small outboard motor onto the stern of the skiff. An Evinrude, I think I remember. So with nothing in mind I started it up and headed down-bay, fully happy I wasn't rowing.

I wasn't afraid. I had become so used to the safety of the bay wrapped around by Jamestown and Dutch Island that I hardly paid attention to where I was going.

Until I suddenly realized I had left Beavertail Lighthouse far behind and could no longer see shore. I was way out in the Atlantic Ocean. There had been a storm the day before. The wind had calmed to a mere whisper and the sea was almost glassy calm. But where there had been big waves there were now huge leftover swells.

Great rolling things that took my skiff up and up and then down and then again up and down. Over and over. And all the time out of sight of land.

That's when I was suddenly hit by fear. What on earth was I doing way out there?

Suppose the little Evinrude conked out? Suppose the little skiff sprang a leak? Suppose some giant fish—suppose, suppose.

Suddenly scared stiff, I took a blind chance at direction, turned around, and headed to what I thought was back to the mainland. And was more than relieved when my guess at direction proved right. Phew, there it was, Beavertail Lighthouse. With the Evinrude still running nicely, I headed for it and took a course that took me up the bay and passing right by it.

That's when I saw the dog. A dog? Yes, a dog. A dog clinging to a rock about a hundred feet offshore from the lighthouse. A rock completely surrounded by the swirling waters of the big swells.

No, it couldn't be. But it was. It was a little hound dog, like a fox hound, but smaller, more like a beagle. How on earth had it got there? A big swell washed over the rock and it disappeared, but there it was again clawing frantically to stay on the rock.

Sometimes you don't think. You just do. I found myself steering for the rock, and then almost on top of it, the skiff hurled at it by a big swell.

I can't remember reaching for the dog, but I did, and the next thing I knew I was on the floor of the skiff, clutching it to me and in silence save for the sound of waves crashing on the rock. The little Evinrude had quit running. The skiff was awash with water. But afloat. And I had oars, so I rowed. You can bet I did. And didn't stop rowing until I was well past Beavertail Lighthouse.

I thought to beach on Jamestown Island and ask around if anyone had lost a little dog. It was a wet, skinny, half-starved she. But decided she was too far gone to have recently had a home. So I took her back to Saunderstown and Grandma, who wasn't happy to have such a flea-ridden animal in her house, and made me keep her locked up in one of the horse stalls, where I made a nest for her and brought her food and water.

I named her Eliza, after a girl rescued from a famous shipwreck centuries before, then and took her back to Garrison when summer ended and turned her over to our stable master, Jack Masters, where she found a warm welcome, sleeping next to him on his bed at night.

And for years afterward, you could hear

Eliza baying after deer in the nearby mountains there, far, far from the rock off Beavertail Lighthouse.

ADVENTURE FIVE

Newport's Own Rat Pack

S till summer, and Bayard and I still at Grandma's in Saunderstown. We decided one day it was time for us to have a look-see at the famous social resort of Newport, a grand place on the mainland across a narrow section of Narragansett Bay from Jamestown Island.

I don't know how or why Newport had become famous, but it was. Very, very wealthy people had built magnificent homes there in the 1800s, palaces almost, and all the uppity social world spent their summers there, with the harbor filled with the most expensive fancy yachts imaginable.

And it wasn't hard to get to. You took the ferry to Jamestown and from Jamestown another shorter ride by ferry into Newport

Harbor and the town itself.

So with Grandma's blessing and Grandpa's also, although he didn't like anything about Newport and all its wealth, we stocked our skiff with sandwiches and rowed down around Beavertail Lighthouse and up into Newport Bay.

That took a whole day, and by the time we got there, we were beat and decided to simply spend the night on Jamestown Island itself and explore Newport the next day. Knowing very little of the island, we rowed up-bay from the town with its ferry slip to where it seemed easy to beach the skiff and use it as shelter at night. Ignorant that we'd beached on the edge of a tidal swamp, we pulled the skiff up off the beach onto what we thought was dry land, turned the skiff over, and propped it up with an oar. We lit a campfire and settled down under the skiff for the night, the lights and sounds of Newport suddenly seeming very far away.

I had hardly gone to sleep when I heard Bayard muttering and using every curse word he'd ever picked up. "Scram, beat it. Get off me you blank-blank-blanks. Scram, out of here."

And then I felt the cause of his anger.

Rats—monstrous big ones.

Squirrel size. They were on me too, running around over the heavy blanket I'd covered myself with. My chorus of curses joined those of Bayard. I got an arm loose and furiously brushed away at least four rats. Big ones, swamp rats that didn't listen to "No. Scram."

And so, that was our night out camping, and fighting rats.

But there was more to come in our daytime excursion of Newport itself, which began with our fleeing the swamp, getting the skiff back down into the water, and rowing fast to get out of there.

We thought.

Before landing in the town of Newport itself, we cruised around its harbor, looking at the many very grand yachts moored there. All of them were big sailing vessels dwarfing Grandpa's little sloop. It was before motors really came in, remember. Vessels powered by motors had arisen, with many crossing the ocean, but very few were owned privately.

It wasn't long before we realized we were disapproved of by some, if not many, of the yachtsmen. It was morning and some were having their coffee up on deck. One, in particular, a still pajamaed man along with his glamorous blond wife, seemed particularly disturbed. His yacht, a big converted two-masted schooner, had attracted us the most, and we circled it twice, ogling, much to his annoyance.

"Hey, you kids. Get lost," and other angry shouts as he got so annoyed that to our amusement he spilled coffee all over himself.

That's when, amidst our laughter, it suddenly happened. There was a rustling movement from under the heap of blankets and camping stuff we'd put in the bow of the skiff. And the next thing we knew, a big water rat had appeared from hiding.

Bayard acted fast. He stabbed at it and shoved it into the water with an oar, but he wasn't fast enough. Two more rats appeared and in a flash, swimming about between us and the big fancy yacht.

And then, those horrible rats sought refuge away from us. Finding themselves now completely exposed, they ran up the mooring ropes of the yacht and onto the deck. The yachtsman cursed and leapt up. His wife screamed.

Forgotten, we beat a hasty retreat in case we harbored more rats, and I guess to hide our laughter.

▼
———— ————

A Different Kind of Grandma's

Right across the Waterway from Grandma's, and just a few yards up a slight rise, was Grandma's barn and stables, a big ramshackle building. Its two stories of shingles were weathered like Grandma's house. It proved to be a world of its own and kept us busy when wind and rough seas kept us off Narragansett Bay.

Stables? It was still mostly horses back then, remember. And yes, stables, first of all. Grandma had hardly graduated from horse and buggy to a first Model T Ford by our second summer. Both Ford and buggy were parked in the barn section, which was dominated by a huge stuffed moose head, which I guess Grandpa had once shot. It looked down

DAVID OSBORN

on them from the back wall.

The stables were four box stalls, two facing two, across a small open dirt courtyard attached to the main building. This proved a near perfect playground for Bayard and me. Grandpa had a big set of painted lead soldiers, hundreds of them, and lying on the ground in that ideal open space, we waged incessant war with them in huge bloody battles, between Napoleon and the British at Waterloo.

Behind the barn and attached to it were two small rooms that were occupied by Farney Gould and his wife. Farney was the lobsterman whose little lobster boat we heard every morning on first awakening, chug-chugging up and down the bay near us.

Above the garage, the horse and buggy, and the moose's head, there lay a surprise that threw a whole new light on our grandfather, Grant. Scores of extraordinary photographs littered the low-ceilinged area. He was a photographer, and an extraordinary one, taking pictures in an almost unheard-of way. He'd pick a subject, a beach, an orchard, a house, set his camera up on a tripod, and then come back the next day at an hour when he judged the light was just right for the shot. Long after

Grandpa Grant was dead, his photographs were discovered and given an important post-humous exhibition in New York's Museum of Modern Art.

Crazy as it seems, both Bayard and I had been plunked onto horses at the early age of three. The horses were ponies but larger than the famed Shetlands. By the time our summers in Saunderstown came around, we rode as though born on horses. And, of course, our parents rode endlessly, our mother famed in the horse show world, our father belonging to some fancy fox-hunting crowd.

And so part of our annual summer move to Saunderstown was a day-long trek by our stable master, Jack Masters, once a champion English jockey and cavalry trooper, towing a horse van with three horses in it. A shrimp of a guy befitting his jockey past, he had come to us during the worst of the Depression look-ing for work when his supervisor job at the Rothschild's racing stables in Canada failed.

That meant that riding in Saunderstown summers was nearly as important as being out on the bay. But ride where?

Bonnet and Beach

L et's get started on the Waterway. Beyond the end of the Waterway lay open countryside, a mile of wild blueberry bushes and wildflowers, then the Bonnet, a huge mass of rock.

Unlike any other part of the coast, the Bonnet, as it was called, was the neck of an extinct but once fiery volcano and was inhabited only by rabbits and the occasional stray sheep. It was a big, towering, unnatural blob that stuck out of the coast and into Narragansett Bay right where the bay emptied into the Atlantic Ocean.

Beyond the Bonnet? A mile of a beautiful empty beach that one day would be a crowded summer playground for thousands.

That was to come in an everchanging world, but back then, the beach was for us a fabulous ride with horses. We endlessly raced them along the sand and into the water where it was shallow. Nobody stopped us. It was ours and ours alone.

Leaving the Waterway, we rode through a half mile of blueberry bushes and wildflowers. A reddish-brown streak was a fleeing fox right in front of us. A whirring of wings, a lark headed skyward from its nest.

We rode up onto the crest of the Bonnet, with its view of all of Narragansett Bay that was so familiar to us: Saunderstown itself with its ferry we had ridden for free, Dutch Island where we had encountered big guns, a blinding searchlight and the incredible kindness of a gruff old Army sergeant, Beavertail where I had impulsively rescued half-starved little Eliza, and where answering the haunting sea chanteys of Angolese fishermen we almost lost Fides, then Newport Harbor, with its rats terrifying wealthy yachtsmen.

And finally, the many wonders revealed in Grandma's barn and stables.

With all of the forever enduring memories of that one wonderful summer in the Saunderstown of my childhood, we turned our horses and started down off the gorse and wildflower strewn Bonnet for "our" mile of white sandy beach.